Ancient Egypt

Secrets Explained!

The Influences Behind Egyptian History, Mythology & The Impact on World Civilization.

By
Jeffrey Houston

©2016

Contents

Prologue

Buried amid the shifting sands of Northern Africa are the monoliths of a once great civilization. For over three thousand years it held power along the lengthy, narrow corridor of the Nile River. Egypt brought a powerful, unified government to a world of anarchy, it introduced technological innovations that were far ahead of its time, and it absorbed through conquest the enemies who would attack it. As Egypt dealt with the day to day events of life, it also delved into the darker mysteries of death and the afterlife.

In school we are taught about Egypt. We are given the radiant synopsis of this great people. We are taught about how they developed a form of writing known as hieroglyphics, which are a set of pictures meant to represent words or ideas.

We are taught about the development of papyrus, a paper made with reeds from the Nile. We learn about the various Egyptian gods. But the fun stories are the ones that deal with Egyptian mummies, many who come back to life.

We hear about brave explorers who plumbed the depths of the Pyramids and found magnificent treasures. We learn stories about curses that were placed on these treasures of the pharaoh, and the grisly deaths of the grave robbers who violated their sanctity. Because of the focus placed on the entertaining aspects of Egypt, much of that ancient civilization's history is a mystery. What historians have learned has been gleaned from pictographs etched into rocks that have suffered the erosion of several millennia. Much of it is conjecture, and much of it is supposition. Very little of what is known has come from recorded texts; time has stolen most of those from us.

So the story of Egypt, as it is known, is shaped largely by what they left behind. Today, what remains of Egypt is the evidence of death.

The Pyramids soar into the sky, colossal three-dimensional triangles composed of over five million blocks of limestone. They are the iconic image of Egypt, and they are also an iconic image of a mausoleum.

They were the burial place of the pharaohs. These Egyptian leaders spent their entire reign constructing the building that would house them in death, committing the mass of the Egyptian population to the undertaking. Death pervades the mythology of the ancient Egyptians, and most of the deities have duties dealing with death as well as their other official function.

The impact of Ancient Egypt is also seen on the cultures that came into contact with it. The Jews, Romans, Christians, and various other groups who interacted with the Egyptians developed strong concepts of a life after death. Although it was not the sole concept to be exported to other nations, it was the one that had the most profound impact.

Egypt was one of the first civilizations to develop on earth. As such, it would make many contributions to mankind's understanding of the world.

But it was Egypt's fascination with death that would provide mankind with knowledge unparalleled in the ancient world. This work intends to study the Egyptian obsession with death and the afterlife, and demonstrate how a civilization with such a morbid curiosity could so profoundly impact the living lives of man.

In order to begin this study, it is necessary to understand the belief structures of the people being discussed. To understand this civilization of the dead, we must look to their gods who champion eternal life.

Egyptian Mythology and the Cult of Death

In order to understand a people, it is essential to understand the most fundamental tenants of their underlying belief structure. It is what prompts an individual to act a certain way, it is what causes a community to develop a set of values, and it is a tradition that becomes passed down through the generations. Because it becomes the most striking facet of a people, the best way to understand their motivating factors is by analyzing their core beliefs.

In the ancient world, most societies developed a polytheistic religious structure in order to explain the world around them. Across countless cultures, through several nations and myriad tribes, the same beliefs pop up. There is a god of the sky, responsible for the ever changing winds and weather that effect mankind on a daily basis. There is a god of the seas, who controls the vast bodies of water on earth. There are gods of love, of war, of fertility, of the harvest. And in every culture, there is a god of death.

The god of death is responsible for the maintenance of the soul in the afterlife.

In many cultures, the admittance or experience of an individual on passing into the afterlife is determined by the deeds, both good and bad, that they performed in their lives.

 The god of death serves as the final judge of a person's life, and is the final decider of one's experience in death. Nearly every culture on earth has a deity similar to this one; Egypt was no exception.

In Egyptian mythology, there existed a pantheon of gods who were in control of the arid lands surrounding the Nile River Valley. There was Ra, the Egyptian god of the sun which blazed down on the desert every day. There was Nut, the Egyptian god of the sky responsible for the changing weather. Set was the god of the desert, and his power was abundantly felt every day. And there was Amun, the god of creation, the one who had brought all things into being while he himself existed outside of the realm of existence.

Though these many gods would occupy the daily lives of the ancient Egyptians, there are several who stand out in Egyptian lore. These will be the gods this study focuses on, as they are the gods who have a strong association with death and the afterlife. This study will look at the roles played by Horus, Sobek, Anubis, Isis, and Osiris.

Egyptian Gods

Horus

To most Egyptians, Horus was the god of the Pharaoh. He was a kingly deity whom the living pharaoh embodied, and in later Egyptian mythology he was associated with being the god of the sky. He was also the god of war and the god of hunting. As a god, Horus bore the head of a falcon on the body of a man. His eyes were said to be the sun and the moon, and the falcon manifestation represented his dominion over the skies. Horus was the child of the gods Isis and Osiris, who will be discussed later as they are part of the Egyptian cult of death.

He was the brother of Set, and the two famously did not get along. Their conflict would be used to describe the constant battle between the people of Egypt and the merciless sands of the Sahara.

Death surrounded Horus on several levels. In the first instance, he was the son of the god of the dead, Osiris. It was this ancestry to Osiris that propelled Horus to his place of prominence in Egyptian Mythology. He was a direct link to the afterlife. In fact, Horus was so closely linked with his father Osiris that while the living pharaoh was perceived as being Horus, the pharaoh became Osiris when he died.

It was with this eye to the future that caused the pharaohs to undertake such a great enterprise as constructing the pyramids. The pyramids were built at a colossal cost in order to ensure the pharaoh had everything necessary in the afterlife. This was not done simply for his creature comforts. The Pharaoh was a living god; as he transitioned into the afterlife he would need a residence that suited his godly status.

As Horus, embodied in the Pharaohs, prepared for the afterlife, he also served as the god of the hunt and the god of war. Both of these were ways for young Egyptian men to distinguish themselves and demonstrate their valor to the people.

They were also ways for young Egyptian men to die. Before entering into either of these two ventures, prayers and sacrifices would be made to Horus to ensure success. But as one of the supreme gods, Horus could not always answer the prayers of these young Egyptians. As such, men were killed on the hunt as they stalked prey like lions, hyenas, and hippopotami. As they encountered their enemies on the field of battle, many Egyptian soldiers died in conflicts that either ended in victory or defeat. Horus had to make these tough decisions for the people of Egypt. As such, he played a pivotal role in deciding life and death. When hunters and warriors prayed to Horus, they were essentially praying for their safety, hoping that the son of the god of death would not offer them up to his father.

While Horus was powerful, he was also a known quantity. He was not only the god of the pharaoh, but he was the pharaoh himself, essentially trapped in a human body. The Pharaoh was divine, and would occasionally shed his earthly form, and the Pharaoh/Horus would assume a new visage. That was understandable to the ancient Egyptians; after all, why would Horus want to keep an old body when he could assume a younger, more vibrant one? In addition to that, death was a risk that anyone assumed when they went out on the hunt or when they went to war.

It was the risk of death and their triumph over it that demonstrated the gallantry of an individual, showcasing their martial skills and their quick reflexes.

Those who failed were not necessarily cursed by Horus. Rather, they lacked the above listed qualities, and were not worthy of the honor of success. In that regard, the Egyptians accepted Horus' role in meting out death.

But not all gods were as well understood as Horus. Some gods lived and thrived by chaos, and were responsible for the random, unexplainable acts that occurred. In Egypt, perhaps the best representation of this deity is Sobek, the god of the Nile.

Sobek

As with Horus, Sobek was an Egyptian god with many attributes. One of the most notable is his lordship over the Nile River, the single thing that determined life and death in Egypt. He was represented in human form with a crocodile head, his teeth exceedingly pointed as a way to demonstrate his ferocity and viciousness. Despite this, Sobek was also an important god who aided Horus in granting the pharaoh his power; Sobek gave the pharaoh control over the Nile River, hugely important for any leader attempting to keep his people happy. Given his fierceness, he was also worshipped as a god that could help with war, as well as the hunt. In many ways, Sobek and Horus were nearly identical in responsibilities, and it was this kinship with the son of Osiris that caused Sobek to later be added into the Osirian legend.

The Nile River provided life for more than just the Egyptians. As one of the only notable sources of water in North Africa, the Nile carved a meandering channel of green amid a landscape of monotonous brown. The Nile provided life to other tribes of people, and it provided water for the plentiful herds of desert animals. It also provided the home of one of the most fearful of Egypt's animals: the crocodile. Lying in wait beneath the murky, mud churned waters the crocodile would wait for any unassuming prey to venture too close.

From animals that needed to drink or cross the Nile, to people who ventured too close to the water to wash their clothes, the crocodile was undiscerning in his taste. He was simply looking for his next meal.

To ward off this fearful animal and the sudden, unexpected death that erupted from the waters, the Egyptians would pray to Sobek. As merchants would set sail up and down the Nile, they would beseech Sobek for safe travels. As the pharaoh consulted his generals about warfare, he and his priests would pray to Sobek to imbue the Egyptian army with the strength of the crocodile and make the soldiers fierce and bold. Sobek held great sway over the Egyptians.

Perhaps the greatest reason for the sway that he held over the Egyptians was that the Nile River was his. Although he didn't control the annual flooding – that power belonged to the god Hapi – the Nile was believed to have been created by the sweat dripping off of Sobek's body. It was the fluid from this god that was able to make the land of Egypt fertile and allowed the people to survive the desert environment. If it had not been for his life giving perspiration, there would have been no Egypt.

For this reason, the ancient Egyptians mummified crocodiles in a similar manner to the way they mummified the remains of the dead. In an ancient city called Crocodilopolis, mummified remains of adult crocodiles have been found, some with young crocodiles placed protectively in their mouths. This was not done to show the crocodiles eating their young, but rather caring for their young. Unlike many reptiles, crocodiles care for their young in ways similar to mammals. By placing the young in the mouths of the adults, the Egyptians were showing both the fierce and caring nature of their river god. They were illustrating the role that Sobek played over life and death in ancient Egypt.

Horus and Sobek are gods with similar attributes, both playing a major role in the lives of the Egyptians. Both also had the capacity for death. But these were not the Egyptian deities of the dead, despite the profound impact they had in that arena. In the realm of the dead, no other Egyptian gods play a stronger role than Anubis, Isis, and finally Osiris.

Anubis

Although not the god of the dead in Egyptian mythology, Anubis is typically the deity conjured up when one thinks of the Egyptian afterlife. The reason for this is because Anubis is the god of embalming and life after death. As Egyptian culture grew and developed over its three thousand year course, Anubis would at times supplant Osiris as the god of the dead, specifically during the period of time known as the Middle Kingdom, which spanned from 2055-1650 BCE. He came to be known as the final judge, the individual that would determine whether or not an individual could pass into the next life, weighing their lives on a scale that determined their human qualities.

As a god, Anubis was represented as a man with the head of a jackal. The jackal was chosen because the ancient Egyptians would often see these animals digging up the graves of the dead.

Unlike the jackals who fed on the dead, digging up their shallow graves to scavenge the remaining bits of flesh, Anubis was the protector of tombs. As he ushered people into the afterlife, he was also responsible for maintaining the sanctity of their eternal burial site, which was typically located on the western bank of the Nile River towards the setting sun.

The name of Anubis would be invoked by the pharaohs as their bodies were laid to rest, both in the Valley of the Kings and within the Great Pyramids. Egyptologists have found many examples of the name of Anubis being etched into the stone of these final resting places. But keeping the earthly bodies of the dead safe was only one function of Anubis.

Another was embalming, an important part of Egyptian life and one that is largely unique to the ancient world. While most ancient civilizations burned their bodies, or simply returned them to the earth from whence they came, the Egyptians took burial a step further.

They developed an elaborate process through which the organs of the dead would be extracted from their various body cavities. Long hooked needles would be inserted through the various orifices of the deceased. Once hooked, the organs would be removed from the body and placed into jars called "canopic jars." These organs would be buried with the rest of the body to ensure that the body of the deceased person remained in one place. They had to be removed from the individual, however, because the juices that resulted from their decomposition could ruin the process of mummification. The only organ not to be removed was the heart, as it was believed to be the center of a person, where their feeling, their intelligence, and their self, existed.

After the body had been washed with wine and the water from the River Nile (Sobek's sweat), and the organs removed, the body would then be dried out with natron, which is a form of salt. This salt would help preserve the body and prevent it from decaying into nothingness. The rags used to treat the body would then be inserted inside of it, taking up the places left empty after the organs had been removed.

This process took forty days. At the end of that point, the body would once more be washed with wine and water from the Nile.

The natron rags would be removed from the body's cavities, and the dehydrated organs would be reinserted. The body would then be packed with sawdust and leaves to give it an appearance of being "full," or normal. The deceased would then be rubbed down with good smelling oils to make the skin appear vibrant and lifelike.

Once done, the individual would be entombed. Throughout the process the priests performing the rites of embalming would have been praying to Anubis in an effort to preserve the form of the dead pharaoh. Anubis would act as judge of the pharaoh's deeds, and decide whether his body would or would not be preserved for the afterlife. When placed into the tomb, the name of Anubis would once more be called on to safeguard the burial site.

Once the body had been embalmed and placed in the tomb, Anubis would be ready to perform his next duty. He was the guide to the dead, leading them into the spirit world and on to the life that existed beyond this life. Anubis was the Guardian of the Scales, the scales being used to determine the goodness of a person. In the Egyptian Book of the Dead, Anubis was seen to weigh the goodness of an individual against an ostrich feather, which represented truth.

If the soul of an individual was heavier than the feather of an ostrich, that soul would descend into the horrific parts of the afterlife and be consumed by Ammit, the Egyptian deity that represented death. Ammit was part lion, part crocodile, and part hippopotamus – all the animals the Egyptians feared. She was not worshipped like other gods; she was Death itself. She would consume any soul that did not adhere to the concepts of truth and justice. The souls who survived the weighing by Anubis were then escorted to a heavenly paradise.

Of all the gods in Egyptian mythology, Anubis is the most portrayed, etched as he was into the walls of tombs. Of all ancient Egyptian structures, it has been the tombs that have been able to weather the millennia, serving as the last linking vestige between the past and the present. Whether it is because the sands of time have eroded a preponderance of other gods, or if it is because he truly was so important, all modern day Egyptologists have to go on is the empirical evidence demonstrating the importance of Anubis as the keeper of souls.

Anubis was undoubtedly important to the Egyptians and their fascination with death. He protected their burial sites, he helped preserve their earthly forms, and he helped guide them into the afterlife.

But despite this importance, he was not as important as two other deities, famous for their marriage, their struggles, and their offspring. To the Egyptians, the story of Isis and Osiris is the story of their nation. It is the story of their struggles as a people, and it is the story of the fate they found themselves resigned to. There are many powerful gods in the Egyptian litany, but none more captivating than this husband and wife.

Isis and Osiris

To the Egyptians, Isis was a pivotal deity. In ancient Egyptian, her name literally translated into "throne," and she was portrayed as a woman with a throne atop her head. She was represented as the seat of power for the pharaoh, and as the mother of Horus, it was directly from her that the Pharaoh was given life and power. Isis was the goddess of mothers; she was the goddess of wives. She was the goddess of nature, and the goddess of magic (things that couldn't be explained) and healing. She was portrayed as the goddess of the downtrodden, but she was also worshipped by the wealthy. Along with Anubis, Isis was a protector of the dead. As the supreme mother figure, she was also seen as the goddess of children. She was one of the first offspring of the earth god Geb, and she would marry her brother Osiris.

Osiris was many things to the Egyptians. He was the first born son of Geb, the god of the earth, and therefore brother to Isis. In the beginning of the Egyptian Creation story, Osiris became the king of the people. In the ancient texts it was related that the people had been cannibals, feasting on one another. On becoming their king, Osiris had introduced agriculture to them, and commanded them to stop eating one another.

Because he brought order out of the chaos, Osiris was also seen as the god of civilization, causing the Egyptian people to rise above the ranks of ordinary animals and become people. Following the conflict with his brother Set, god of the desert, Osiris would die and be reborn. Because of this, Osiris the king becomes lord of the Underworld. He is typically portrayed as a mummy, painted either black or green to indicate death, and he bears the crown, flail, and crozier that are associated with Egyptian pharaohs. In Egyptian traditional stories, Osiris marries his sister Isis.

This marriage was pivotal in the stories of creation told by the ancient Egyptians. According to the ancient mythologies, Osiris was the eldest son of the earth god Geb. Set was his younger brother.

As often happened, the younger brother Set grew jealous of his brother. Osiris was a wise ruler. He was a champion of civilization, a well-loved king, and he was married to their sister Isis. In his jealousy, Set devised a plan to kill Osiris. One night, as Osiris slept, his brother measured the size of his body.

The next day, Set hosted a banquet for in his brother's honor. He wanted to pay homage to his worthy elder brother, and it was during this feast that Set offered a great prize.

He had crafted a beautiful box, and said that whoever could fit perfectly within it would receive the box as a gift. Everyone at the banquet attempted to fit inside, but the box had been built specifically to Osiris' specifications. As the good king climbed into the box, Set closed the lid on the box, effectively trapping Osiris inside. The chest was then filled with molten lead, killing Osiris instantly.

With Osiris now dead inside, Set cast the coffin into the Nile River hoping that the waters would carry the body of his brother far away. But in her devotion to her husband, Isis searched far and wide for his coffin. Ultimately, she found him off the coast of the neighboring civilization of Phoenicia. She brought the body of her loved one home, where she could grant him a proper burial. Before she could bury him, however, his body was discovered by Set. In a fit of rage, Set cut the body into several pieces, casting them across the earth to prevent Isis from bringing them together again.

But Isis was the goddess of wives for good reason. She was devoted, she loved her husband, and with the help of her sister she was able to track down all of the pieces except for one: Osiris' penis. As the pieces of his body had been scattered, his penis had fallen into the water and was eaten by a fish. Unable to retrieve all the pieces, Isis was able to use her powers of magic to fashion a golden penis for Osiris. She then put all the pieces together. Osiris, who had been killed, had been brought back to life. Using his golden penis, Isis assumed the form of a bird and conceived Horus.

Osiris had died and been resurrected. This in turn had given him the power over death, which in turn had given him the power over death. However, though he came back from the dead, he did not possess enough life to remain among the living. So Osiris travelled back down into the underworld, where he was given dominion. He was assured that his son Horus would in turn rule over the living. Thus from birth and into death, the people were ruled over by Osiris and his son.

Osiris was not alone in the underworld, however, as it was also the dominion of Anubis. Anubis had been born the child of Set and Nephthys.

Set was unwilling to have a child with her, so Nephthys disguised herself as her twin sister Isis. She succeeded in seducing Set, and as a result the god Anubis was born. Fearful that she would be found out, however, Nephthys pleaded with her sister Isis to adopt the baby. Isis did, and Anubis became part of the family of Isis, Osiris, and Horus.

For the Egyptians, the tale of Isis and Osiris was important because it showed that life did not end in death. Instead, the ancient Egyptians perceived death as merely a transition between two phases of existence. Provided they lived a "good" life, they would receive immortality similar to Osiris. They also saw this cycle of death and rebirth in other facets of their lives.

Osiris was the god of agriculture. In conjunction with Hapi, Osiris was seen as the Egyptian deity responsible for the annual flooding of the Nile, resulting in the silt deposits that replaced the nutrients in the depleted soil. Following the flood, a new batch of crops grew, and the Egyptians were able to feed themselves. Then the crops would die, and the waters would recede. Osiris had emerged from the underworld brining life, and when he returned the fields fell fallow.

The roles played by Isis and Osiris were pivotal for the ancient Egyptians. In fact, when analyzing the marriage of these two gods more closely, and looking at the roles of their offspring, every aspect of Egyptian life was presided over by them. An Egyptian was born to a world where Horus, the son of Isis and Osiris, ruled over Egypt in the guise of a pharaoh.

Horus and Sobek gave the pharaoh his power, and Isis and Osiris gave him the authority to rule. The food that was eaten by all Egyptians was guaranteed by Osiris, and the life giving waters provided by Sobek. When an individual was sick or wounded, then Isis would answer their prayers and heal them. As Egyptians died, they prepared their souls to meet Anubis and Osiris, and traipse through the underworld into the afterlife, where they would experience a new beginning.

This is but a small glimpse into the lives of the ancient Egyptians, but it is a powerful glimpse at how much the concept of death figured into the daily lives of this great people. The Egyptian preoccupation with the great beyond does not stop with their religious beliefs. It can be seen everywhere archaeologists have explored in the sand covered nation. For Egypt, death was so intrinsically linked to their society that the majority of the remains of their civilization were built with death in mind.

Architecture of the Afterlife

When you travel to Egypt to see the classical sites, everyone knows what you'll see. The Pyramids. The Sphinx. The Valley of the Kings. They are visited because they are largely all that remains of this once vibrant civilization; the rest has been swallowed up by the shifting sands of the desert, and eroded by wind and time. They are visited because they are there, standing as colossal reminders that a civilization once existed there. They are there because they are unique, belonging to a time when the world was ruled by gods instead of God, when the resources of a people could be put to work to engineer such massive structures, and when pharaohs ruled with the divine right of gods. These are the earmarks of Egypt, elements that separate them from the rest of the classical world. And they are buildings that were constructed in a celebration of death and the afterlife.

The Pyramids

Up until the modern era, when mankind learned how to develop steel and other lightweight materials that could support tremendous weights, the Pyramids had been the largest structures on earth. The pyramids have been the subject of countless conspiracy theories, given their awe inspiring size as well as the countless peculiarities that exist within them.

When looking at the pyramids, it is easy to get lost in the scale of them and look at them with the appreciative eye of a modern-day snob congratulating the industrious workers of the past. It can be easy, amid conspiracy and mystery, to forget that these massive structures are tombs.

Pyramid building began as long ago as 2639 BCE, in an area called Saqqara. The pyramid was built for an Egyptian king named Djoser (pronounced Joe-sur). At the time, typical royal tombs were rectangular rooms built into surrounding rock. These tombs were called mastabas, and were intended to provide everything the Egyptian King would need in the afterlife. As Djoser ruled, he assigned an architect to design and begin construction on his tomb. The designer he hired was named Imhotep.

Imhotep had designed the temple with the idea of ascending into the sky. Steps represented an ascent, and the pyramid was designed to assist the pharaoh return to heaven so that he could enjoy his afterlife. It was a vast undertaking, using mud brick that would be made out of a combination of mud and straw, which would then be stomped by the workers. Then, brick by brick, the Egyptians would build skyward.

For over twenty years Egyptian laborers toiled and worked on Djoser's tomb. Eventually, they had created a stepped pyramid. Like a layer cake, where the lowest level is the widest and the tallest level is the smallest, the pyramid climbed 204 feet into the air. At the time of completion, it was the world's tallest building; but the Egyptians were just getting started.

After Djoser, stepped pyramids became the norm, with each one being built to a size and scale exceeding the one before it. With each construction, attempts were made by the architects and the builders to build a design truer to the concept laid down by Imhotep. He wanted to create a building that gave the appearance of the rays of the sun so that the pharaoh could ascend to heaven and join the gods, primarily the sun god Ra.

Eventually, this construction was completed with the Red Pyramid at Dahshur, the first pyramid that had smooth sides.

Eventually, this would be copied in Giza with the construction of the Great Pyramid. Built for the pharaoh Khufu, it is the largest pyramid in the world. Each side is 230 meters long, and the height is 147 meters. His temple consists of over 2.3 million blocks of limestone, with each block ranging between two and thirty tons. Some records indicate that it took a force of over 100,000 men twenty years to build the pyramid.

When it was completed, the pyramid was finished with a smooth layer of white limestone casing stones that reflected the sun. When looking at the top of the pyramid, it seems to be missing the tip. As far as recorded history can relate, the pyramid has always been without a capstone, which has led many archaeologists to speculate about what may have been at the top. Some say a triangle of pure gold, others have speculated about a gigantic orb designed to replicate the eye of Horus.

Oftentimes lost in the grandeur of this and other pyramids is the fact that it was built as the final resting place for a man, his family, his servants, and his earthly belongings. Everyone knows that the Pyramids contain the King's Chambers, where the sarcophagus of the deceased pharaoh was placed and all his worldly possessions piled up. The pyramid, for all its size, for all its magnificence, is a tomb.

It was designed to be a portal for the Egyptian pharaoh, to help him transition easily into the afterlife. The outward display of pomp and circumstance was nowhere near as important as the function of the interior.

In order to assist Anubis with safeguarding the chamber of the King, the individuals working on the pyramid created an elaborate system of tunnels and traps, designed to prevent anyone from attempting to steal the royal treasures of the pharaoh.

The walls were engineered so precisely that not even a sheet of paper can be slid between them. Some walls within the pyramid were designed so that a worker could move a 20 ton slab of granite with a push of a finger; then, once set in place, no discernible outline of that swiveling door can be seen.

The Great Pyramid at Giza was designed with precise specifications in mind. Of all structures from the ancient world, it is the one most exactly pointing north. When lined up, it falls in the exact geographic center of earth (the other exact center point is located in the Pacific.) Mathematicians rave at the engineering of the Pyramids, of the ancient's use of Pi, Phi, and of scale representations; the earth is 10^8 the mass of the pyramid, and the internal temperature of the pyramid is the same constant as the earth at 68 degrees Fahrenheit.

According to some Egyptologists, all of these things were done to assure the pharaoh's safety in death, to place him in the center of an object that perfectly represents the earth over which he holds dominion.

Aside from serving as the eternal vessel of the pharaohs, the pyramids have had a profound impact on our modern study of Egypt. They are a few of the remaining Egyptian structures, and as such they contain most of the information we have on ancient Egypt.

As the tombs were opened and explored, a complex system of writing was discovered on the interior walls, typically describing the life and deeds of the individual interred within each pyramid. Though at first impossible to discover, and ancient stone known as the Rosetta Stone was discovered during Napoleon Bonaparte's invasion of Egypt.

On the stone was a combination of Egyptian Hieroglyphics, Demotic Script, and Ancient Greek. This discovery opened a school of study, Egyptology, allowing modern researchers to decipher the meanings of the pictures painted on the walls of the Egyptian tombs.

Had it not been for the incessant need to prepare for the afterlife, for the preservation-minded priests and their need to make sure everything would be ready for the pharaoh in the next world, the pyramids would not have been the vault of knowledge they became. Given their immensity and their seemingly never ending tunnels, researchers have consistently been able to build a story of Egypt's past. This process has also been helped by the relatively newer discovery of the Valley of the Kings, a necropolis (city of the dead) of Egyptian royalty and valuable source of historical information.

The Valley of the Kings

In an area to the west of the Nile in the Theban hills, there was an unassuming valley. Not as grandiose as the pyramids, not as visually appealing, the Valley of the Kings was nonetheless some of the most sacred ground to the ancient Egyptians. As Egyptian civilization moved forward in time and faced several threats, both foreign and domestic, the capacity to build such massive stone edifices slowly diminished. In addition, the Pharaohs were from different parts of Egypt, and no longer necessarily wanted their remains buried in Giza. Many began interring their remains into vast underground tombs.

Because the individuals being buried were royal, the interiors of the tombs were still spectacularly decorated. Massive facades decorated the entrance to the tombs, clearly indicating which pharaoh was buried where. As with the pyramids, elaborate measures were taken to protect against tomb robbers. Unlike the Pyramids, which required vast numbers of laborers to move the quarried stones from miles away to Giza, everything the tomb builders needed in the Valley of the Kings was there.

The Valley of the Kings is the home to some of the most memorable of Egypt's pharaohs, including the lineage of Ramses the Great. As with the pyramids, workers spent the entirety of the pharaoh's life preparing his eternal resting spot. Great care was given to the decoration of the interior walls, where extensive hieroglyphics were painted detailing the passage of the soul from the land of the living into the underworld. In order to help the soul reach the afterlife, the priests in charge of the pictographs would spell out in detail the route the soul must take so that it wouldn't be lost. Other parts of the wall spelled out the deeds accomplished in life by the deceased; all which were intended to help them gain entrance to the afterlife.

Unlike many later religions, the Egyptians were not expected to be perfect. In some cases, when the soul stood before Osiris, the person would have to give a detailed accounting of things they did not do to demonstrate their overall decency.

Because the network of burial chambers is much more intricate and much more populated in the Valley of the Kings as opposed to the pyramids, much of what is known of ancient Egyptian society has come from the necropolis. Although more of these tombs had been ransacked by looters, resulting in the loss of precious antiquities and valuables, the walls were largely ignored as they could not be sold. The wealth from the Valley of the Kings comes not from the treasures that were discovered, but the irreplaceable knowledge found on the walls of the tombs.

What is important to note is that most of the information that has been gleaned on this ancient civilization has come from its tombs. The history that we know of Egypt is largely a history of preparing for the afterlife, due to the simple fact that these are the few structures that haven't been destroyed.

We know that the Egyptians placed a heavy emphasis on the afterlife; we know this primarily because most of the history of Egypt that we know comes from stone mausoleums.

In large part, our view of ancient Egypt is heavily biased, based solely on the availability of data. The case for this argument can be seen by our understanding – or lack thereof – of the Sphinx.

The Sphinx

Not every monolith in ancient Egypt has a story to divulge. As archaeologists unearth long forgotten cities, they are faced with conjecturing what life might have been like for the ancient Egyptians based off of the artifacts they find. In some cases this can be extremely helpful in understanding the past; in other cases it can be completely erroneous. One such object that has been studied for countless centuries is the Sphinx, perhaps the most mysterious ruin of ancient Egypt.

The Sphinx is 73.5 meters long, 19.3 meters wide and 20.22 meters high. It is located near the Great Pyramid on the Giza Plateau in Egypt, and it is the oldest known sculpture in the world. That is what is known about the Sphinx, and that is where contemporary knowledge of the structure ends.

To this day, no one knows who built the massive half-man half-lion. Some in the historical fields argue that certain elements of the design and the placement in regards to the second Pyramid at Giza indicate that it was built at the time of the Great Pyramids, but other historians contend that the erosion and the aging shown on the Great Sphinx indicate that it predates the pyramids.

There is no writing on the Sphinx, which has caused the archaeologists responsible for its preservation to infer its purpose. Some have hypothesized that, like the Pyramid and temple complexes surrounding it, the Sphinx and its temple are memorials to a long distant pharaoh whose name has been forgotten with time. Others have speculated that the Sphinx served as an indicator, a device marking the rising sun of the Spring Equinox. They believe this was done as the sky was moving through the Age of Leo, and that the shape of the Sphinx is evidence of that.

That is as much as modern science has grasped as it has probed the mystery of the Sphinx. Because of its mysterious nature, many conspiracies surround it. Some claim that the Sphinx contains a secret vault housing the documents of ancient Atlantis. Others have claimed that aliens constructed it out of sand as a marker. In the absence of any written evidence, all that can remain is conjecture, which is dangerous when pursuing scientific truths. Any and all attempts to probe the depths of the monolith have failed, leaving more questions than answers.

It is for these reasons that most look at the reclined Sphinx and conjure a different story. Perched as it is on the plateau near the Great Pyramids, many see the mythological creature as a guardian of the pharaohs entombed behind him. For most Egyptologists, given the colossal scale of the building at Giza, they feel comfortable giving credit for the Sphinx to the pharaoh Khafre. Many see the Sphinx as a manifestation of the god Anubis. As the god responsible for protecting tombs, this association can easily be understood.

The reason it is important to demonstrate what archaeologists have learned from the Pyramids and the Valley of the Kings compared with what they have learned from things like the Sphinx is to show the startling difference. With the Sphinx, there are no records. There is no tale, no story explaining its significance. There is no history graven onto the mass of sculpted limestone. Conversely, the Pyramids and the tombs of the Valley of the Kings are flush with written records. They involve detailed stories about the individuals entombed within; they demonstrate an intricate system for passing into the afterlife. When it comes to understanding ancient Egypt, the only serious records that archaeologists have to study are infused entirely with death and the afterlife. It is almost as if the only things worthy of note in ancient Egypt are the records of the dead.

Legacy of Egyptian Beliefs

Throughout its lengthy, tumultuous history, Egypt did not stick to itself. At the height of its power, Egypt was actively engaged in warfare against neighboring civilizations. As its power began to wane, Egypt was assaulted from various sides by younger, upstart civilizations. Wherever it ventured, and whoever it came into contact with, Egypt left a lasting impression. Much of what is known about Egypt has been gleaned from the practices that other cultures had adopted as a result of their interaction.

Some of the best known examples of this cultural diffusion are the precursors to modern day Judaism and Christianity. It began with Judaism. In that religion's holy book, the Torah, the second book is called Exodus in reference to the flight of the Jews from Egypt. According to the Jewish text, the Jews served as slaves to their Egyptian masters, performing back breaking manual labor as they struggled to build the pyramids. In that book, the tale is recounted of a young man named Moses who was born and destined to one day lead his people to freedom. As he matured, he became close to the pharaoh and his first born son, almost as if he was an adopted member of the family.

Moses eventually embraced his destiny and helped lead his people out of Egypt. He did this by accomplishing ten miracles with the assistance of God. The Egyptian priests attempted to refute his miracles by performing magic of their own, magic given to them by the goddess Isis, but in the end Moses' God proved to be more powerful. Following a massive plague wherein the firstborn of every Egyptian house was killed, the Jews were permitted to leave Egypt. As they left, the pharaoh chased them, and Moses caused the Red Sea to split. When all the Jews were through, the waters came crashing down, and the pharaoh and his men were swallowed by the waters.

The Egyptian impact on the Jews was so profound that it is essentially the story of their origin. They perceive themselves as a struggling race, as a civilization that had to cast off the shackles of servitude. The primary differences between the faiths rest in the nature of god; the Egyptians believed in a supreme god with several lesser gods who nonetheless were extremely important. The Jews believed in a single God. Both groups believed in the existence of an afterlife, however, although the path to reaching it was profoundly different for both groups.

For most of the classical world, the impact of the Egyptians rested in its sciences and mathematics. The Greeks and the Romans, as they encountered the Egyptians on the other side of the Mediterranean, perceived the magnificent scale of Egyptian construction. Both cultures picked up on elements of mathematics which the Egyptians had mastered thousands of years before those fledgling civilizations even began. This classical style of antiquity was seen in both Greek and Roman architecture. Much of what they modeled their structures on stemmed from buildings such as the massive Pyramids, the extensive Valley of the Kings, and other Egyptian curiosities.

Another area where ancient Egypt contributed to the classical world was in the realm of medicine. Isis, as one of her many domains, was the goddess of healing. Egyptian doctors were very advanced for their time, as was the Egyptian scientific community. They had the time to develop these skills, especially as they were one of the first civilizations to emerge on Earth.

In both Greece and Rome, there emerged a cult of Isis. In Egypt she had been revered as the mother of Horus, and therefore as the mother of the Pharaoh.

She was seen as a powerful, nurturing force herself, and the Romans and Greeks added her to their own list of deities. Her worship in these Western nations was heavily secret, filled with secret rites that did not survive time. In the beginning, it was known that only men could be priests in the worship of Isis, but overtime women were allowed to lead the worship ceremonies as well. The adherents to the cult of Isis were notable for shaving off their hair in Egyptian fashion. Though it made its way to the Greece and Rome, the cult of Isis largely maintained its Egyptian qualities.

Perhaps one of the more profound impacts made by Egyptian culture was in the religion of Christianity. Derived as it was from Judaism, there are also several elements of Egyptian mythology that are paralleled in Christianity. When reading through the New Testament, the books that are Holy Scripture the Christians the world over, the reading begins with the birth of Jesus. Then, suddenly, Jesus appears on the scene as a full grown man; as he has grown, he has travelled to Egypt. Once he returns, he begins performing miracles. He heals the sick, causes the blind to see, raises individuals from the dead. He begins to establish a following based on what he preaches.

It is likely that in his travels, many of the religious beliefs of the Egyptians were imparted on the young Jew from Galilee. According to the Jewish faith, the Jews were the chosen people, and therefore the only ones who could ascend to Heaven. Jesus denounced this idea, and claimed that heaven was open to all who believed in him. In the Christian faith, the message is all about Heaven, about suffering through the world, about living a just life, and being rewarded with eternal bliss. Much like in Egyptian mythology, souls of the individual are judged at the end of days, and found worthy or unworthy for passage into heaven. As with Egyptian mythology, there is an expectation for how an individual should behave in life. If their sins are too heavy, they will not gain access to the afterlife and will instead be devoured by Satan.

Throughout the Christian doctrine, there are many parallels between Jesus and Egyptian mythology. In the Christian faith, Jesus is seen as the son of God, with the power over death. This is paralleled in Horus, who is the Son of Osiris, the god of the afterlife. In the Christian faith Jesus is born to Mary, who is a virgin. In Egyptian Mythology, Isis is able to conceive Horus through her magic, due to the fact that the penis of Osiris had been devoured by a fish loyal to set.

In Egyptian Mythology, Horus is the pharaoh, and is the king of all kings. In Christianity, Jesus is the king of kings. In Egyptian mythology, the symbol for life and resurrection is the ankh, which is in the shape of a cross with a rounded head. To Christians, the cross is the symbol of Jesus' crucifixion, and his ultimate resurrection from death. To the outside observer, there are countless similarities between Egyptian Mythology and Christianity. Most of them have to do with death and the soul's life after death.

It is nearly impossible to describe in detail the many aspects of our modern day world that have been impacted by the Ancient Egyptians. The truth is that the history of ancient Egypt lasted longer than the amount of time that has passed since its collapse. In an effort to put the duration of ancient Egypt into perspective, two facts deserve to be mentioned. The first is that Cleopatra, famous Queen of Egypt who fell in love with the Roman Marc Antony, lived closer in time to the creation of the first Pizza Hut than she did to the building of the Pyramid. If that doesn't put the age of Egypt into perspective, perhaps this next fact will. When the Great Pyramid at Giza was built, Wooly Mammoths still roamed the world.

It is impossible for a culture like Egypt, which endured for so long and came into contact with so many nations, not to make some kind of lasting impression.

The most notable impacts would be on the belief structures of the nations it came into contact with. By the time most modern civilizations emerged, Egypt was fading. The Nile River Valley was shrinking; crops were smaller than they had been. The great wealth of Egypt wasn't as great as it had been, and the pharaohs weren't capable of such elaborate building projects as their forbears. Egypt was assailed on all sides by new civilizations, each seeking to gain access to the fantastic riches of Egypt. As a result, most of what they came into contact with was a civilization on the decline.

As civilizations around the Mediterranean moved into the spaces once occupied by Egypt, they were encountering a dying nation. They moved into homes that held little significance, they made no effort to preserve the records of the daily lives of the Egyptians. They took what they wanted, primarily wealth and knowledge, and slowly but surely subjugated the civilization that had once held power over most of the known world. They made their way to the crowded cities of Egypt, they beheld the wonders that we still behold today.

They borrowed that architecture and incorporated it into their own, not truly understanding that they were fashioning buildings in the shapes of mausoleums. They listened to the Egyptian mythologies, hearing stories and taking with them the ones they found most enjoyable. In some cultures they added these stories, or added elements of them, into their own faiths. For most, they enjoyed the element of the afterlife that was missing from their own religion. Many civilizations began to cling to the tenant of life after death, and began trying to live in a just manner so as to gain access to that afterlife. Over the millennia, the seeds of Egyptian culture were spread around the Mediterranean world. In turn, those cultures have spread around the world. Every culture existing today contains some element of ancient Egyptian belief.

Epilogue

Egypt is a land of myth and mystery. It is a land as old as history itself, as some of the first forms of writing on earth emerged within this ancient civilization. It is a land with a complicated past, with a compelling history that cannot be summed up with one book, let alone a series of books. It is a civilization that is still slowly divulging its secrets to modern day researchers. As a civilization, it has forgotten more of its past than other civilizations have experienced. Tragically, this is the problem faced by Egyptologists today; most of Egypt's past is buried in the shifting sands of time. It is a past they are painstakingly seeking to find.

As researches search for clues to unlock the hidden secrets of Egypt, there are few reliable sources they may turn to. The houses in which Egyptians lived have crumbled with time. Countless wars of conquest and religious changes have destroyed any oral tradition that may have existed. The Egyptians who live in Egypt today share nothing with their ancestors of the past except for blood. So, in order to piece together the story of Egypt, researchers must turn to the dead.

Egypt is a land of the dead. It is a land where existence is never guaranteed. The scorching heat and dehydrating aridness of the desert are a constant threat. The land close to the rivers is patrolled by some of the deadliest animals on earth. When their civilization was at the peak of development, ancient Egyptians had to contend with the torrential flood waters of the Nile. The river they relied on for life so easily brought death. The ancient Egyptians were surrounded by death. Rather than give in, they found ways to deal with it.

The Egyptian mythology is filled with gods and goddess, many of whom play a central role in the acts of death and the afterlife. Of all the gods represented, it is the deities that deal with death that tend to hold more power in the pantheon of immortals. Isis and Osiris take center stage, although Ra is the god of the sun, Geb is the god of the earth, and Amun is the supreme god of creation. Through Isis and Osiris, the daily needs of the Egyptian people are met. Through their son, Horus, and through Sobek his adoptive brother, the pharaoh gained his power and was able to lead his armies to conquest throughout northern Africa. Their other adoptive son, Anubis, served as the guide to the underworld, where he would usher souls forth to meet his father, Osiris, the god of the dead. The cult of Osiris, as it came to be known, became a powerful force in ancient Egypt, a force whose precepts many people lived their lives around.

As they spent their life waiting to transition into the afterlife, the ancient Egyptians found ways to entomb and preserve their bodies, ensuring that the soul was never cut off from the body until it was ready to proceed into the underworld. For those wealthy enough, massive stone edifices were erected to safeguard their remains from the jackals of the desert, and the jackals of mankind. Because of the care spent in creating these works, Egyptian history was preserved in much the same way as their bodies. It is through inscriptions on tomb walls where researches have been able to piece together most of the pieces of what is known about ancient Egypt.

As a culture, Egypt did not remain isolated. For several thousand years it expanded across the deserts of North Africa and into the Middle East, following the Nile to its source and vying for complete control of that waterway. Along the way, the most lasting impression left by the Egyptians was their culture. It would impact more than one nation. Much of early Jewish and Christian traditions stem from practices first established by the Egyptians. The Romans and the Greeks, with their polytheistic religions like the Egyptians, were eager to incorporate elements of Egyptian religion into their own.

In this way, much of the Egyptian heritage was preserved for posterity; researchers are able to understand ancient Egypt through its contact with other nations in areas where there is no distinguishable evidence in Egypt itself.

In a land as harsh and uninviting as Egypt, it is easy to see why the people looked with such promise at the afterlife. There, an endless garden with cool waters awaited them, as opposed to the grainy sands and dangerous waters of the Nile. There peace awaited them, for only those whose soul was lighter than an ostrich feather could enter heaven. From the moment of their birth they were conditioned to prepare for death; it was the only thing that made surviving in ancient times possible, especially in the desert. But rather than fear death as the last unanswered question, as the long enduring night, the Egyptians embraced death, confident in the fact that something else waited for them on the other side. For the Egyptians, death was merely the next step in life. In order to meet it, they would spend their lives preparing for it. When it came they embraced it, knowing there was nothing to fear.

Thank You

Thank you for purchasing this book, I hope you have a greater understanding of Ancient Egypt and the belief and influences of this great civilization.

If you have enjoyed this book, why not explore the wonders of Greek Mythology, with my book;

<u>Greek Mythology, Gods & Goddesses Explained!</u>

Thank you.

Made in the USA
Monee, IL
19 November 2021

82541644R00031